This Notebook Belongs To

____